RUNNING THROUGH THE DARKNESS

The Story I Don't Want To Share

UNFAZED PUBLISHING
YOUR MIND IS OUR BUSINESS

Tampa Florida

MARCUS L. BOSTON

MARCUS L. BOSTON

ISBN: 9781-959275-26-8

Library Of Congress Number: 2023935522

UNFAZED PUBLISHING
YOUR MIND IS OUR BUSINESS

Marcus L. Boston

Making The Church

A Better Place

Introduction

I share my story for people who are unbelievers. I'm sure your reason for reading this book will differ from other readers. You're probably curious, or maybe someone convinced you to take a look at this. I used to be an unbeliever and I was anti-Bible. I argued and fought with Christians openly at Hillsborough Community College Ybor Campus in Tampa Florida. I honestly do not desire to share this story. Most people share their death and near death stories with joy and happiness. I share my story out of a need for it to be shared; so here it is.

I love Jesus and I'm so grateful that God released me out of hell when I didn't know Him. However, I was looking for God. There are too many ministers who proclaim much too often that people in the world are not thinking about God or looking for Him. They say they were enjoying sin and focused only on pleasure. Well, I was enjoying my sinful life, but I was looking for God. I've always believed God existed because of my childhood experiences, but I didn't always believe the Bible. To those of you reading this book, who do not believe the bible and hate Christians, I was you. I pray for your souls often. I pray this story helps you believe that the Bible is the Word of God, and that Jesus Christ is the Son of God.

<u>Table Of Contents</u>

Chapter One
My Unusual Supernatural
"<u>Childhood</u>"

I do not remember my exact age when these things began, but once it started, it never stopped. As a very young boy, maybe 3, 4, or 5, I saw many things and I shared them with my mom. The most popular one you've read before in several of my previous books. I'll share this first. I used to see a man in my closet. I was not asleep nor half sleep. I was wide awake. I tapped my mom to wake her up. She asked me what I wanted. I shared, "Mom, there's a man in the closet." She told me there wasn't a man in the closet. I said yes there is. She kept saying there wasn't a man in the closet. I was looking right at him as we went back and forth. My mom rose up, turned on the lights, walked into the closet, and looked through the clothes while I watched. There was no man while she did this. As soon as she turned the lights back off, there he was and she was very frustrated with me. She went back to sleep and I stared at this man in the closet who also starred back at me. Many nights I couldn't sleep as a young boy. I would be up all night scared and terrified of the things I saw in the darkness.

One night I couldn't sleep and I called my father to come pick me up. I do not know what time it was, but my mom was already asleep. He came and took me to his apartment. He went right to sleep and I was up wide awake. He had some music playing on his radio that was from his childhood. He played this music every time he went to bed. His favorite singer was Perry Como. He loved jazz and big band. As he slept, I looked out into the darkness and was hoping I didn't see anything scary. I had no peace. I do not know how long it was that he slept, but I tapped him, "Dad, can you take me home?" My father rose up and took me back home. He wasn't angry or upset. He didn't even ask me why. I wondered about this night many times over the years.

Once I was back with my mom, I couldn't sleep again. I do not know how long I was up, but I called my father to come get me again. Guess what? He came and got me. He wasn't angry or upset. He didn't yell at me. He was quite patient, and once again, he didn't say anything or look as if he was angry. This time at his apartment, I fell asleep. My dad passed in 2005. I wish I could ask him about that night. Why did he come and get me twice? Why was he so patient? What was going on surrounding my life that I wasn't knowledgeable concerning? You know, I've never sought the Lord about this night, but I now wonder what is my backstory enveloping my conception and birth.

There were nights for a few weeks when I

began hearing noises on our floor. I stood up in the bed and turned on the light. I saw several rats scattering as I observed them. I remember our apartment being clean. My mom would mop the floor and it would be so shiny. I was told with boldness, "Do not walk on my floor! Wait until it dries." I remember my sisters cleaning up as well, along with my grandmother who stayed with us sometimes. We did have some roaches. It wasn't a lot of them, but I do remember seeing them sometimes. However, we did have rats for a season. I would hear them running around as I laid in bed. Fortunately, I could stand up in bed and pull the light on. I wasn't scared of the rats, I was scared of the man in the closet. I believe my mom had pest control called because the rats were soon gone. Maybe the rats were a supernatural sign in some fashion. I shared all of this because of the things I'm going to share next.

My cousin was staying with us and on one occasion, he witnesses something very shocking. I was staying with my dad when this event happened. There was a bad rainy thunder storm that night and my cousin who was a little boy a year younger than myself, said he saw a giant crab come inside our apartment through the window. He ran out of that bedroom and closed the door shut. He then heard some very loud noises inside the bedroom. He didn't go back inside of that bedroom. The next day when everyone gathered for breakfast, my cousin shared what he saw. No one believed him of course, but something would be seen that would possibly change their minds. The bedroom where the loud noises took place and where the giant crab was supposed to be, would finally be entered. The door remained closed until one of my sisters entered. What they found was very shocking. The steel fan was destroyed. It was bent up, broken, and could no longer function. It was beyond the ability to be repaired. No one wanted to admit a giant crab did this, but everyone agreed that someone strange definitely took place. Chicago doesn't have any oceans and no crabs are in the Midwest. I've heard this story shared several times throughout my life and I shared this by memory only. My cousin has no recollection of this event. He really doesn't remember it, but I've heard this story many times. I wasn't shocked at all hearing it because I've seen many things that were unbelievable. Let's move on.

Most nights when I could go to sleep, I had nightmares or dreams of having sex. Let's talk about my nightmares first. The nightmares were me fighting monsters and in these dreams I always won. I could fly, I was very strong, and I could do many amazing things. In these dreams I was fighting monsters of all sorts from giant ones to small ones. Sometimes they fought me in groups. I had these dreams throughout my childhood, my teen years, and as a young adult. I was never killed in any of these dreams or eating by them. Whenever I had sleep paralysis, I would wake up prior to them finding me. There were plenty of these dreams that were very intense and I would wake up exhausted. There was one particular nightmare I had as a teen where a monster chopped up my hand and I woke up with small open papercut looking wounds on the same hand that was chopped up. These dreams were a way of life for me and I thought everyone had these dreams too. Moreover, I thought people saw monsters while they were wide awake like myself. I now understand these monsters are demon spirits. I learned to stop talking about the things I saw because people started looking at me as if I was weird. After I became a Christian, I began sharing the things I saw again, and a prophet told me to stop sharing what I see because people think I'm crazy. This is when I learned that all Christians do not see in the spirit realm; which leads me to another topic, "Horror Movies."

As a child, I saw a few movies that I'm sure my parents who have not allowed me to see. Back in the 70's, it was easier to keep things secret from children and protect children from information they shouldn't be exposed to. However, I was a child left alone at times. At the age of 7 I was baby sitting my first nephew. Yeah I know you're probably surprised. Generation X are made different. I was cooking my own breakfast at age 6. I learned very quickly to cook bacon on a low fire after the grease popped on my forehead and burned me. No tears, no crying, no running to momma. During these times I was left alone, sometimes I watched television unsupervised. Most of the time I found some cartoons, but depending on the time of day, I watched things I shouldn't have viewed. I remember seeing a movie on "Svengoolie", "Son of Svengoolie", and Elvira Mistress Of The Dark that added to my nights of terror. Movies such as The Blob, The Howling, Trilogy of Terror, and Zombie had me up all night in fear. There were several others, but these are the ones I remember off the top of my head. Images of the things I witnessed in movies were in my dreams and I saw them outlining darkness. Because of everything I experienced in my childhood, I knew the spirit world was a very real place. No one had to convince me.

There were nights when I watched tv alone when I would see someone watching me in my peripheral vision. When I turned over to see who it was looking at me, they slowly faded away before my eyes. There were times I saw people walking out of my bedroom while I watched tv in my mom's bedroom. These people were not scary and they didn't seem as if they didn't like me. I was very sure they weren't trying to hurt me. However, there was one particular night that was the absolute scariest.

I was in bed with my mom who was asleep. This is the night the man in closest came out of the closet. I was jumped over my mother and ran through the darkness to where my grandmother was sleeping. I jumped over her into her bed. She rose up looking over at me briefly and laid back down. She went right back to sleep without asking why I jumped into her bed. Grandma's bedroom was dark, but the bathroom in the nearby hallway light was on. I left the door wide open and the light shined dimly inside of the door. I heard the man in the closet walking very slowly down the hallway. "Boom"... "Boom"... "Boom"... "Boom"... "Boom." I was wide awake and looked at my sleeping grandmother in great fear. I was on the inside of the bed right next to the wall that separated me from the hallway the man in the closet was walking through coming after me.

As I heard him walking down the hallway, he suddenly stopped. I turned my head facing the wall. It's as if I could feel him on the other side staring at me. I started trembling. I knew he was coming for me. "Boom"... "Boom"... "Boom," the sounds of his feet hitting the floor began again and stopped again. This time I knew he was standing outside of the open bedroom door just out of my line of sight. I stared at the dim light on the wide open door. I could feel him standing there as if he was hunting me. Out nowhere he appeared in front of the wide open door without making a sound. My eyes stretched wide in fear. His outline was the shape of a man and an animal together. He was darker than the darkness of the bedroom. After receiving his image within my eyes, I threw myself down on the bed pulling the covers over me. As soon as I pulled the covers over me in fear, I quickly sat back up! It was the next day and my heart was beating exceptionally loud as I breathed rapidly wondering how did day come so fast. My grandmother was not in the bed. The sun was shining bright through the same window the giant crab entered. I was left confused trying to figure out what happened. I do not remember anything after pulling those covers over me. Did the man in the closet get me and I can't remember? (Food For Thought: I've cried 3 times writing this book so far. Twice concerning this event specifically. I suppose this was very traumatic for me and I'm receiving healing as I write. Maybe this is why I don't want to write this.) I hate that I do not remember what took place after I pulled the covers over me. Maybe God has this hidden from me for a reason. Maybe I witnessed something and it's locked away in my mind. Maybe it will be a mystery forever. As a child, this is the scariest night I've ever experienced. In addition, with whomever I shared this story, they experienced this in some fashion. As if this spirit transferred into their life from this story. I rebuked that from ever happening again in the name of Jesus.

Another situation that was scary, but not as scary, was when I was a young teenager. I moved by bed into the basement because it was a hot Chicago summer. We didn't have any air conditioning and the basement stayed cool. One night when I was asleep, I heard a voice calling my name. At first I thought it was a family member pranking me. However, I noticed the light was off outside the door entering the basement. No one would stand there in the darkness trying to prank me. I had a light on so I wasn't in pitch black darkness. It was after midnight and I called out the names of my family who stayed in this house. No one responded. I recall saying, "This isn't funny. Stop playing." No members of my family responded. I laid back down in my bed and that voice called me again. "Marcus... Marcus... Come here. Come here Marcus." I rose up out of my bed and turned the main light which lit up the entire basement. The voice was coming from the back room near the entrance / exit door. Just like in the movies, I got up slowly and started walking toward the voice calling me out of curiosity. I was definitely afraid as I inched my way in the direction of the voice. I grabbed my baseball bat just in case it was an intruder. Then I thought, [What am I doing? This never works out in the movies.] I quickly ran back to my bed, turned the tv on, and stayed up until the voice stopped. I never heard this voice again. Maybe it was a family member playing. Now let's talk about the sexual dreams.

As a child I didn't know it was sex. I was not exposed to sex in any manner, and I was not molested as a child. Television in the 1970s didn't have much sexual content and themes. Most television broadcasts were very family oriented. There was nothing in my life and no one in my life that exposed me to sex. I was too young. Like the supernatural things, once I started having sexual dreams, they continued on a regular basis becoming normal for me. They were very graphic and I didn't understand anything of what was being done to me and what they had me doing. In these dreams, I was still a little boy. I wasn't a teenager or an adult version of myself. I was not having sex with little girls. These females were adults. They were completed naked when the dream began or they took all of their clothing off right in front of me. These women wanted me sexually and were very aggressive.

They French kissed me deeply and took off my clothes. They performed oral sex on me and I saw this clearly. After they were finished, they would lay down and open their legs wide. They instructed me to perform oral sex on them. The women were always very vocal and told me how they wanted it. They were very authoritative as if they were my boss. My little boy mouth was visibly on their vagina. After their body shacked and trembled with the loud noises they were making, I was instructed to get on top of them between their legs. They grabbed my penis and stuck it inside of them. They told me how to stroke. We changed positions in these dreams. There were different women each time I had these dreams. Some were from nationalities that were not black. I never shared these dreams with my mom or dad. As a matter of fact, I never shared these dreams. Many times when I woke up from these dreams, my penis was hurting. I didn't know what an erection was at that age.

I wasn't a normal boy. I've always liked girls. I've never looked at girls as a little boy and was disgusted. I used to always wonder how they looked under their dresses. I ran around kissing girls. I loved playing "Catch A Girl Kiss A Girl," and the only game better was when the little girls wanted to play "Catch A Boy Kiss A Boy." I made sure I was always caught. While the other little boys ran, dodged, and hid from them, I would trip or fall on purpose. I wanted to be caught. I made it easy to be caught. I loved it. Multiple girls were kissing me all over my face was very enjoyable. I used to run around kissing on my little female cousins until family adults explained why I needed to stop; and I did.

One repetitive dream I continued having was so unusual. This dream happened outside for obvious reasons. I would be outside playing in an open field and suddenly, this giant naked woman came to me. When I say giant, I mean giant. She could have squashed me. She was hundreds of feet tall and I was the same little boy. This giant woman wanted to have sex with me and of course, this was an impossibility. Her vagina size was longer than my entire body, but she told me to lick her clit which was bigger than my head. She laid down flat, picked me up, and placed me on her clit. She told me what to do and I did it. When she had orgasms, all of this water came out of her vagina. Being a child I called it water, and her body shook all over as she made loud noises. She had me kissing and licking all over her body in some dreams. When it came to intercourse, my penis couldn't even go inside of her, but my arm could enter and I was scared I would fall inside. She told me what to do with my body parts and when she shook with the water coming out, I would be caught in the flow and washed to the ground. I was never hurt when I hit the ground from the fall, and my entire body would be soaked with her water. None of these dreams were wet dreams. My first wet dream was at the age of 12. I had a porn magazine one of my friends gave me, and I looked at all of these naked women prior to going to bed. I dreamed that I had sex with this stunning white woman I viewed in the magazine. This was my very first orgasm. I still didn't know about masturbation at this present time in my life. I woke up in the middle of this orgasm and I remember how good it felt. It was so good and I honestly hoped it would happen again. I loved this feeling. Nonetheless, this was my childhood. Now let me tell you about my family, and my friends, the things I witnessed of them as being Christians which helped me hate the Bible.

Chapter Two
"<u>Enemy Of The Bible</u>"

Well, I was not in the church much as a child. I have a few memories that were nothing special in my opinion. The verse train up a child in the way he should go is not my story. I recall going to a church that was under the CTA L tracks in Chicago and I hugged this lady who was sitting in a chair. I'm told this was an aunt that really loved me. I have no other memories of her, and I don't recall anything else at this church. At my grandmother's house, dad's side, I recall walking to a church with my family. I remember it vaguely, but do not remember anything else. Around the age of 7, my mom took me to a church that had overnight service. Literally, from night until the next day. I don't recall exactly because I went to sleep. I don't remember the preaching, but I do remember a few songs they sung. I do remember somethings that I was told to never mention to people. I did however tell my dad about night service at this church and he was very angry. He confronted my mom and they had a huge fight. I was present and it was ugly. So ugly that I ended up living with my dad. While staying with my father, we never went to church, but he did take his mother to church every Sunday and picked her up from church every Sunday. I rode with him. I remember going to church with my grandmother one time. I do not remember anything other than sitting inside during the service and eating food in the nearby room after the service ended.

I recall going to Vacation Bible School which only lasted a week. This church was right across the street from my grandmother's home. I remember going with my cousins, but I do not remember learning anything. I was that kid sitting in the back not paying attention. I do not recall anyone their making sure we children were paying attention. I do remember my aunts and grandmother praying together in the living room. One time they made us children stand with them as they prayed. They were all into it. After they prayed, they would talk about the prayer and at times, talked about spiritual things. I remember a few things they talked about. You'll hear about all of these things I remember later in this book.

At some point I started living back with my mom. One day as we were sat together in the upstairs living room, a bird flew inside our home through the window. It flew inside the window and circled several times. The adults started grabbing things to get make it go back out through the window. Once this bird was outside, all of the adults stopped and looked at each other in fear. I was 9 or 10 years old. I looked at them as they looked around at each other. They all looked afraid for some reason. Finally, someone said, "Oh

my God! Someone is going to die tonight!"
Then there was silence. I was confused as a
child because I wondered why would
someone die because a bird flew into our
home. Those words stayed with me. I
remember praying that no one died in my
family. I always believed God existed as a
child and I prayed sometimes. The next
morning I rose up early, and many adults
were already up. Death did happen in our
home that night. I went into our basement to
find 1 of our 2 puppies dead. Even though I
was sad about it, at least it wasn't a human
that died. There were other events such as
this that happened, and I remembered these
situations as I grew older.

Once I moved back with my mom, she no
longer took me to church with her; neither
did I ask to go. These began the days when I
no longer went to church at all. At the age of
16, my mom moved us to Tampa Florida. My
mom went to church on Sunday and I didn't

go with her. I was invited to church by one of my white friends at King High School. It was on a week night and I walked to this youth service. I attended, but I do not recall anything. He invited me again, and I went a second time. Once again, I don't remember nothing at all. I didn't come back again. I was invited to church by several other of my friends at high school, and I went. I was invited to a Kingdom Hall and I went. I had a girlfriend who's mom was a minister. They invited me to church and I went several times with them. After I graduated high school, I had a girlfriend who invited me to church and I went. The last time I went to church was with my boy Alfonso. We partied all night and I was too tired to go home so I spent the night. The next morning Fonso's mom asked us if we wanted to go to church. Fonso asked me and I agreed to go. All I had on was the clothing I partied in the night before. When we arrived at church, Fonso's grandmother says to me, "We don't where that in church!" She said this with an attitude and I had a mouth on me. My only response, "Fonso! You betta get your grandma!" He grabbed me to make me keep walking. I was so offended and I sat in church angry the entire time. I do not remember anything from this church service. I couldn't wait to leave and whenever I drove passed this church, I got angry just looking at it.

I mentioned only one name from my friends because the friends I had that went to church weren't the best Christian examples. I didn't drink, smoke, get high, or curse much. This had nothing to do with the Bible. Many people in my family acted a fool after drinking. Many of them cursed all of the time. Many were on drugs etc.. I just didn't want to be like any of them. The friends that invited me to church got drunk, smoked, got high, cursed etc.. When I started Hillsborough Community College in January

1991, I was an unbeliever. With all the things I witnessed in my family and with my friends, I had no confidence in the Bible. The thing that was very shocking to me about myself is that I was very angry at Christians. This anger manifested in the Cantina as I passed a group of individuals debating the bible. I joined this debate against the Christians. It became very heated and I cursed, "Get the fuck out of my face with that bible!!!" As I argued against them, I suddenly remembered one of them. "I remember you! You was at the club! Getting drunk!..." That Christian immediately got quiet because they were guilty. The other Christians shut up for a second as I talked. "Ain't nothing to that bible. Y'all are delusional. Where is the power? Where are the miracles? Y'all full of shit!!! Shut the fuck up!!!" More of the Christians started looking sad and deflated. Meanwhile, those of us that opposed them were slapping high fives and giving each other daps. We celebrated as they tried to recover themselves. Finally, this female Latina Christian started talking about God's grace, but we weren't even listening. We were still celebrating and saying things to each other as she talked. This round was over, and we needed to get to class. We left them and didn't say goodbye. They were still standing there when we exited.

The next round ended just like the first. This time around I was very arrogant and more disrespectful. I don't remember how many of these debates we had on campus, but I was very bold, cursing, and hitting Christians right where it hurts. One particular battle ended on a peaceful note. There was a woman sitting near us as we debated the Bible. She was not in the debate and she sat their reading her Bible. I asked her, "So, what do you have to say about what we are talking about?" Everyone became silent as we all waiting for her answer. She opened her mouth, paused, then was about to say something again, paused and finally uttered, "One day, you will know the truth." We all kinda looked at each other and then I added, "That's all? That's all that you have to say?" "Yes. That's all. One day you will know the truth." She said in a very calm manner. We were all fired up and she was calm. She went back to reading her Bible and we went back to battling.

I fought other Christians off campus as well. I enjoyed destroying them and my boldness grew in our fights. One campus, they stopped fighting against us. Our encounters became one sided conversations. They would sit in the Cantina and talk among themselves. Whenever we came around, they ignored us and left us alone altogether. This made us talk among ourselves in loud boisterous ways so they could hear us. We made sure they heard our negative statements about Christianity, and they never fought us again. Our group of anti-Bible people began to stop communing. We would speak and keep it moving on campus. As the Christians left us alone, we soon left them alone, but we felt victorious against them. We believed they didn't want to talk to us because they lost.

Now that I am a Christian, this is why I join in battles when I hear people attacking Christians. Now I defend the gospel and the Bible. On the back cover of this book, I mentioned Yoruba. With so many people promoting this on social media, Netflix, and with ancestors displayed in Black Panther movies, my experience in Yoruba needs to be shared. It's actually already written in another book of mine "Enchanted." I'll share it in the next chapter.

Chapter Three
"My Yoruba Experience"

Here's what I wrote in my book, "Enchanted." Beginning on page 76 paragraph 1.

I believed that God was real because I had spiritual eyes, but I just didn't believe the bible was true. I started looking into other religions trying to find God. I eventually met someone and found myself very curious about their religion. She was from west Africa and the name of her religion was Yoruba. I asked several questions when they replied," Let me give you a reading." I've heard of readings and really expected this to be another disappointing experience. She asked me to give her something, and I didn't understand what she asked me. Then she asked, "Give me a penny. Do you have a penny? I need something with your energy on it." I gave her a penny. She took the penny and added it to something that looked like shells with a few other things that I had no knowledge of. She started speaking something as she took all of those items together and began shaking them and turning them as I looked on. She finally threw all of these items together on what looked like a special made plate of some kind. She gazed at these items for several moments as I sat silently waiting to hear what she had to say.

Very peacefully she proclaimed, "You have psychic powers. You are a psychic. This is why you know things, and don't understand why you know them. (I nodded because that was true.) I see that you've had some mysterious deaths in your family. (I had no knowledge of this so I'm looking very doubtful.) I see you getting pulled over by the police, but don't worry. It's nothing."

I didn't think much about this reading she gave me. However, I talked to my mom later that day and asked her, "Have we had any mysterious deaths in our family?" She shocked me with a yes response to my question. Then she went on explaining all of the mysterious deaths. I couldn't believe that this woman was right. In addition, later that night I was pulled over by the police and as they looked at me dressed up in my car they said, "This isn't the car. You can go." This african priestess was right.

Since she was right I went back for another reading. This time it was something very serious and because she was right the first time, I took heed to what she told me. "Your father is sick and he's not telling anyone about it. He's not taking his medicine either. I hate to say this but if he doesn't take his medicine he's going to die." Now this reading embraced my thoughts. I kept thinking about this reading until I had to call my father on the phone. I knew I couldn't tell my father the truth so I told him this. "Dad, I had a dream about you. I dreamed you were sick and wasn't telling anyone. Plus you weren't taking your medicine and in my dream you died." My father replied sounding somewhat sorrowful,

"Well son, that's true. I am sick and I haven't told anyone. And... well... I'm not taking my medicine." "Dad, can you please take your medicine please? I want you to be around much longer." I said in a concerned tone. "Ok son, I'll take my medicine. Thanks for calling me. I love you son." "I love you too dad." I happily responded.

After the second reading was correct, I desired to know everything about this Yoruba religion. My dad took his medicine and he lived. Because of what she revealed about my dad I had plenty of questions. I began talking with her over the phone. I began going to her home just to hear about Yoruba. One by one she began teaching about the different Orishas. It was a lot to learn, but I wanted to know. I asked her about the setup she had near the front door of her home. She explained that was an altar to the Orisha that she served. I remember one day when she was going outside into her backyard and I saw another altar. This altar was much bigger and I asked her about it as well. This altar was for animal sacrifices. I was confused for a moment. She saw the look on my face and started laughing. She explained how she offered chickens, pigeons, and goats on the altar. She then asked me if I was busy, and I wasn't, so she asked me to accompany her as she went to the store. Now when she said store, I was thinking grocery store. She took me to the store where she purchased live animals for sacrifices. I wasn't even aware such a store existed. She purchased several animals that she had delivered to her home.

Because of how much I had learned from her she asked me, "So, are you interested in being in my religion?" I said yes, but I wanted to know more before I made a decision. She was pleased with the answer I gave her and invited me to attend one of their Yoruba ceremonies. I honestly had no clue what was going to happen at this ceremony. She didn't prepare me in any wise for what I was going to experience.

When I arrived at this location, I was excited and looked forward to seeing what I might learn. Once everyone was present, they were about to begin when someone asked about me. "Who is this? What is he doing here?" An african man said with curiosity. She replied to him, "He's with me. He's interested in joining us. He's learned a lot so far and I invited him." "Ohhhhh ok. He reminds me of someone. Yes, yes. I see Elegba (also referred to Eleggua or Elegguá) all over him. Elegba wants you to serve him." said the african man to me. She agreed with him and added, "I've told Marcus the same thing about Elegba." Then I just listened to them talk.

Soon they began the ceremony. Lots of candles were lit and the african man burned incense as he began saying things I didn't understand. I felt like I was literally in another world. Then they all started saying things together that I didn't understand. Then the african man started putting a liquid in his mouth and spitting it out forcefully! Then he started saying something in another language. He repeated this several times. While he did this others were saying things that sounded like prayers in my opinion.

After these things everyone became silent for a moment. The african man appeared to be in charge of everything. He started giving instructions. After receiving these instructions everyone was silent waiting to see if something manifests in the midst of us. All of a sudden the incense began to form right before my eyes. I guess I looked as if I was surprised because they all started asking me, "What do you see?" I described what I saw and they explained what was revealed. Then there were other things I saw as well. One person told me, "There is a dark force following you." Then they detailed the image and someone else told me what they meant. I wasn't afraid of anything that I saw and everyone was impressed with the fact that the Orishas manifested things to me in front of them. I wasn't shocked at all with seeing spirits and spiritual things because I've seen them all of my life. I had a lot on my mind when this ceremony ended.

Seeing these different manifestations did make me think that this is the religion that I should join. I had visited many churches with family and friends on different occasions, but I never remember seeing any power moving in these churches. Seeing these different manifestations of power made me start calling some of my friends and sharing what I was learning about Yoruba. Even though I shared the power that moved and the readings that were true, every one of my friends that I shared Yoruba with said they didn't want to hear anything else about it. Some were angry and one was even sorrowful. That part of me that contended with Christians manifested and I even apologized to them. The sorrowful friend really did touch my heart by saying, "Marcus... you need to be very careful... about joining this religion. I've never... heard of it, but I just don't feel you should join." I respectfully responded, "I really do appreciate your honesty. Thank you." I kept those words close to my heart because what my friends say really mattered to me.

During this season of my life I had an enemy. This guy hated me. Every time he saw me he always erupted into anger. He and I almost fought on a few occasions. I decided to get a reading about this situation. The reading didn't make me feel any better, "Marcus, you should avoid fighting this guy. His anger is fueled by rage and he will fight you will that same rage. His dead friend is why he is so angry and even in death his friend's spirit is following him, and aiding him. His dead friend hates you and wants you dead. You can hold your own fighting, but his anger and the help from his dead friend will over power you. You'll end up very hurt. Avoid fighting him."

I didn't want to avoid him; I wanted to fight this guy. But I took heed to what the african priestess told me. I pondered on what I could do. With all the things I learned in Yoruba, I actually used those things I've learned for this situation. I went to the kitchen and prepared an offering for the Orishas. I had an altar in my bedroom and placed the offering on it. I lit my candles and burned my incense. I said those things she taught me to say, I had a piece of paper with my ancestor's names of it, and other things that I won't describe. I made a strong request for the Orishas to keep my enemy away from me. I even told them that I never wanted to see him again. I asked that they didn't kill him, but just keep him away from me. After I was finished with everything, I felt a very strong presence in my bedroom. It was so strong that I actually trembled in fear. I could feel that my request was heard, my offering was accepted, and the Orishas was going to perform what I asked of them.

I went into the bathroom and brought with me everything I used to make my request to the Orishas. I spoke these words, "As I flush this down the toilet, I flush him out of my life forever." I tossed it in the toilet and flushed it.

Immediately, what I tossed in the toilet leaped up!!! It's like it was trying to escape being flushed!!! It leaped almost 2 feet straight up but did not break free of the water, it held its upright position for almost 3 seconds, and suddenly went straight down the toilet!!!

My eyes were stretched open and my heart was racing as I witnessed spiritual power manifested in front of me. After I witnessed the toilet water leap up I truly believed my request was done. I never seen him again. He didn't die, but I never seen him again. I didn't even share this with the african priestess.

I kept learning everything until I finally asked, "So, how do you get into this religion?" She detailed, "Well, you have to be initiated. You will have to shave your head. You will be given a tattoo of the symbol of the Orisha you will serve on your head. You'll be in a dark room for several days alone..." I interrupted her, "...Why would I be in a dark room several days alone?" I interrupted her again before she could explain why, "...So, let's say I get into this religion and then one day... I decide... I don't wanna be in it anymore. Can I just walk away?" "NO!" She practically shouted. "If you walk away the Orisha you dedicated your life to will kill you." On that note I became unsure of what to do and voiced, "Well, I need to think about this before I make a decision." She understood.

This is the untold story of what happened before I prayed my last prayer which is in the Preface of "A Pastor's Mistake." I prayed "God, I believe you exist, but I just don't know how to get to you. I don't even know who to call you. I just don't believe all these religions lead to you. As of today, I am no longer looking for you. But if you give me the truth about you, I'll live it." I've heard too many ministers saying how they weren't even thinking about God while they were in sin, but I was; I was looking for Him. I even feel His presence now as I type. That really makes me feel good knowing I was looking for God although I was in darkness. I believe this prayer took place in April 1993.

Because of signs and wonders I was interested in Yoruba. This is how so many people get into false religions although they were Christians. However, I want to add this: these Christians who have left the Lord for Yoruba and other religions were in dead churches. Dead meaning that the Spirit of the living God did not move within these churches. There is no way you can have an encounter with Jesus and just walk away from Him to serve other gods. Notice in Yoruba; I would have been serving an angel (Orisha) and not God. Moreover, we were honoring and worshiping our ancestors too. After the Lord gave me the truth about Him which was in August 1993, I was so happy once I knew with all confidence that I had the true and living God in my life. After learning what I did in Yoruba was witchcraft, I greatly repented. I repented for everything I did: the altar, the offerings, the tributes I did when I passed graveyards, turkey buzzards, railroads, bodies of water etc.. I repented for what I did when I flushed the toilet. I prayed for that spell I released to be broken and destroyed off my enemy. I loosed salvation and deliverance over his life. After I prayed for him, I ended up seeing him again without any conflicts. I knew then the spell was broken off his life. I was actually happy to see him knowing that he was free and I was forgiven.

About three months later after I prayed my final prayer, I died and went to hell. Long story short. My throat was swollen shut and I couldn't breathe. I died in the hospital. In hell I was chained against a wall. I yelled, "Godddddd!!!!! Please don't leave me in here!!!!!" My chains broke. I was revived in the hospital. I thought it was a bad dream until I read the book, "Divine Revelation Of Hell." I read exactly where I was in hell. I yelled after I read where I was in hell, "That was for real!!!" I threw the book and wept because I was really in hell. Death feels like you're going to sleep. A deep sleep that you can't fight. Maybe I'll write the entire story in a book. Now back to the

Egyptians."

Well, this is the book that will contain the entire story. What you just read from my book, "Enchanted" was written in a very respectful way. There is so much more I could share about Yoruba. However, certain specifics do not need to be shared. What I do desire to say next is this: Yoruba and Christianity are not the same. On the Netflix documentary, this woman was explaining the similarities of Christianity and Yoruba. It's not the same. I'll start with our ancestors. Our deceased family members are not helping us in the afterlife. In my book "Enchanted," I talk about the akashic files. Here's what I wrote: "Another way agents of satan, witches, and false religions obtain information, is the "akashic records." I heard of this in the world, but I didn't look into it. I read about the akashic files/records by reading books by former witches. According to these former witches, the akashic files are in the realm of the spirit. According to former witches, the akashic records are filled with everything about our lives in great detail. Witches can access these records to gain information about our lives in order to launch a strategic attack against our lives. Everything we've ever done is found in these records. Former sins, former desires, former failures, what we like, what we don't like, and everything else is there according to these former witches. Even in their books, the former witches warned the readers of their books to never try to access these records because you need approved demonic access. Without their access, they will attack you. One website said that the akashic records are the book of life mentioned in the bible. I know this is untrue. The book of life is God's book and if your name is written in this book you will live with God forever. "And whosoever was not found written in the book of life was cast into the lake of fire." Revelation chapter 20 verses 15. Now the bible does say the other books were opened. Maybe those other books are the akashic records. Honestly I don't know. "And I saw the dead, small and great, stand before God; and the books were opened: and another book was opened, which is the book of life: and the dead were judged out of those things which were written in the books, according to their works." Revelation chapter 20 verse 12. I don't know about the akashic records, but I do know the bible talks about the spirit of divination. I just thought I would share this information with you." **Enchanted page 113 paragraph 2.**

Our deceased relatives are either in heaven or hell. When I died at the age of 22, which I will share momentarily, I was judged immediately by the life I lived. I wasn't standing around seeing my dead body and wondering what would happen next. That's not my story. People who are saying our ancestors are talking to us are receiving their information from familiar spirits.

Familiar spirits are spirits that run in your family bloodline who know everything about your family. The information provided is from the akashic files. The information is not from your ancestors. Yep, I had a list of all of my ancestors that was on my altar. I gave them offerings on a regular basis and said prayers to them. Just like we should not be praying to dead saints as Christians, we should not be saying prayers to our dead ancestors. Do not pray to Mother Mary, she doesn't hear you. Stop it please. Stop praying to your ancestors. Your ancestors are not hearing these prayers, but the familiar spirits are listening. We pray to God and God alone, in the name of Jesus. All of the offerings to our ancestors are the equivalent of giving offerings to idol gods, and so are these prayers.

I purposely left out certain things within my Yoruba story. As I learned more about Yoruba, I changed. I started wearing African clothing. There was an indoor shopping building in Ybor City called "Ybor Strip." There was a store that sold authentic African clothing. I bought many African garments and it turns out, a few of them were priestly garments. I was sold out until I learned the Orisha I would serve would kill me if I walked away. I also purposely left out how I really met the african priestess. Well, I was dating her daughter and when the daughter introduced me to her mom, well, you know the rest. I brought this up because I want to share something I purposely left out; the dream of her daughter and I.

As I begin to tell you this dream, I want to say that I was in love with this woman. I embraced her family, their culture, and I could see myself married to her. We didn't have any fights or arguments. I thought we were perfect together. Here's the dream:

"I opened my eyes as if I just woke up and said to myself out loud, 'I know this is a dream.

I'm not a slave.' I was dressed as a slave and I knew I was dreaming. I was outside of a barn looking building that was on a huge plantation. The master came over to me and told me, "Boy, pick up that hay and feed the horses in the barn with it." I responded and sounded just like a slave, "No sir massa, I ain't pickin' up nothin.' I's not a slave." Massa responded, "Ohhhhh, so you's a smart nigger, huh?" I nodded my head saying yes without saying it. Then massa says, "Well, since you're such a smart nigger, I'm gonna reward you. Stick your hand out." I wasn't as smart as I thought because I stuck my hand out. Massa took out a machete and chopped my right hand very quickly. Blood shot from my right hand and I ran away from massa. My girlfriend was also a slave and I grabbed her hand with my left hand. She instantly started running with me. "Where do you think y'all going niggers? I own y'all!" Said Massa. As we ran away together, I could hear the dogs behind *us. All of a sudden, my girlfriend tripped and fell down. I let go of her hand and kept running without her. I never looked back."* I shared this dream because my right hand had vertical open cuts when I woke up. This is the dream I shared earlier. My hand was chopped vertically in my dream and my cuts matched. I couldn't have squeezed my hand causing this because it was vertical. If I did it the cuts would have been horizontal. I had what looked like papercuts in the palm of my hand. Very interesting huh? Let's continue.

Because I dreamed my entire life, I knew this dream meant something. Not long after this dream, my girlfriend broke up with me. It wasn't a devastating breakup. Here's what happened: "I wasn't ready for the words she spoke to me in a very sweet, kind, and nice fashion, "Marcus, you are a great guy. You have treated me very well. You're the type of guy I want to marry. (My eyes got really big.) But, I'm not ready to get married. No time soon. I'm not ready for the type of relationship you want with me right now. I wanna be free to do what I desire to do." I was looking so confused as I heard these words. She continued, "I just want you to know I'm very happy with everything you've been to me and the things you've done for me. Maybe we could get back together in the future..." "...Wait, you're breaking up with me?" I cut her off feeling hurt and shocked. She quickly responded with a tenderhearted voice, "No, no, Marcus, you wasn't a bad boyfriend. You were good to me. I'm just not ready for this type of relationship right now. You weren't bad at all. Like I said, you're the kind of guy I want to marry. Please don't feel hurt. Please?" I took a deep breath and said, "Ok, I'll try not to feel bad. I love you though. So, we might get back together in the future? (Yes) Ok. We are now friends and no longer in a relationship." She hugged me and I walked her back home. There's so much more to the story with this woman." (From my tell all book, "From Woman To Woman." Page 99 line 8) After she broke up with me, I continued learning from her mother. I was involved in many activities associated with Yoruba that my now ex-girlfriend, her mom, and family participated in together. I believed the dream was telling me to let her go and move on with my life, but she did it for me. During this time in my life, I had many books on Zodiacs, and I looked up my horoscope regularly. I experienced de-ja-vu quite often and trying to interpret my dreams was a normal part of my life. Let's continue.

The final thing I desire to talk about are the animal sacrifices to the Orisha that you serve. I'm not trying to disrespect this culture and believe system. Yoruba is always painted in a picture to make it look so harmless. It looks so inviting to those of us from African descent. Lots of African Americans are open to learning about authentic African culture. Many of us are ignorant of our history and desire to know the unknown concerning us. There are black people in the Bible and the Bible is not the "White Man's Religion." Everyone in Africa is not in Yoruba.

Animal sacrifices are in the Old Testament, but are no longer necessary because Jesus is the lamb of God who was slain for every nationality of people globally. Jesus is for everyone. Jesus died for every person worldwide. All you have to do is believe it, but believing is very hard for some. I was one of those people and why I'm writing this book to help some of you believe. In Yoruba, those sacrifices are for the Orisha that you serve, or to your ancestors; or both. Sacrifices are often made for them to do a specific task. You can ask for them to do anything; even the unthinkable.

Jesus says to love your enemy and to forgive them. You cannot ask Jesus to do something that is outside of His word. God does revenge evils done to us, but there is a verse in the bible that says, "Rejoice not when your enemy falls, And let not your heart be glad when he stumbles: Lest the Lord see it, and it displeases him, And he turn away his wrath from him." Proverbs chapter 24 v. 17-18. When you desire God to do the unthinkable to someone, He will in turn do nothing. God is graceful, but He's also just. This is why God desires us to forgive and love our enemies. Like I said earlier, Yoruba and Christianity are not the same. I'm grateful I have never sacrificed a live animal, but I gave other offerings on the altar I had in my bedroom. When we give our lives to Christ, our personal life is our sacrifice unto God. We are now made righteous because of His precious blood that was shed for all of our sins. There is no need to shed any more blood. Jesus paid the price. The only issue is accepting what Jesus did for us. We do not need to serve God's angels, dead saints, or any other entity that is lower than God. As a matter of fact, the angel in the bible Revelation chapter 22 v. 6 -9, told John not to worship him because he's a fellow servant like John. We are not to worship angels. We worship God; not angels, not our ancestors, not dead saints, and not mother Mary. (I took the time to correct some things Christians do that they shouldn't be doing Biblically.) Yoruba worships angels and their ancestors. I'm not coming against anyone's culture. This is about your eternal soul. Throughout the Bible, there are many cultures of people who are mentioned and detailed who served idol gods. Most religions made animals sacrifices; including God's followers in the Old Testament in the Bible.

One thing is certain though: I've seen the

power in the Yoruba religion. I'm so happy I've seen the supernatural my entire life. I'm so grateful that I had the mindset to ask that final question. Above all, I'm grateful for that last prayer I prayed to God although I didn't know His name. If you've been in a dead church (Meaning God's presence is not there.) all of your life and have never witnessed the power of Jesus, if you got a reading from someone in Yoruba, you would probably be impressed just like I was. All of us desire to see supernatural power. Let's just be real. Look at everything that is spiritual today in 2023 presently. Too many to name. People purchase spiritual objects because they believe it will do a certain thing they desire. We are captivated when we witness spiritual things. Here's the shocker: there are many spiritual voices and spirits that can speak to us, tell us things that are true, and can perform things to prove their existence. God will do something too depending on what's needed. This is how I became a Christian. God did something for me and I believed the bible was true. Many times God doesn't have to do anything because many people believe without seeing a sign. This is why no one desires to be converted to any other religion because their belief in what they witnessed is very real to them. Coming to someone about Jesus when they have already witnessed supernatural power is like talking to a brick. Look at the Egyptians in the Bible. Moses performed supernatural things and the Egyptians did too. The Egyptians weren't impressed with the supernatural things Moses performed. There are many spirits that can do things to get you to serve them. Jesus appeared to Saul (Paul) because there was absolutely no other way he would believe. I'm telling you that Jesus is Lord by my experiences. Let's continue.

Before I conclude this chapter, my Yoruba

experience has so much more I could add, but I'll stop right here. My last point is a talk I had with my girlfriend before she broke up with me. She stated, "Christians are always talking about Jesus, but what did Jesus ever do for them? They pray and nothing happens. We pray and things happen." I agreed with her with a smile on my face. I was happy she disliked Christians. She told me that her mom used to be a Christian and now she's a Yoruba African Priestess. Let that sink in Christians who are reading this. I can guarantee based on my experience that her mom was in a dead church. Just a bunch of services where God is not present. Just a religious church service with no power, and then you meet someone in Yoruba who gives you a reading. Yep, that's how this happens. Signs and wonders do not always mean its God. For most Christians, you must believe first and see something later. However, there are cases such as mine where God did something specific for my eyes to open to Him. Yes, I said "for my eyes to open to Him." The Bible says that unbelievers are in darkness and are blind. This book is written in an effort to break that blindness off of you so you see the bible clearly. I pray for all unbelievers. I pray your souls are saved in Jesus' name.

Chapter Four
"The Holding Cell"

Well, here is the story I don't want to share. After I prayed my final prayer, *(God, I believe you exist, but I just don't know how to get to you. I don't even know who to call you. I just don't believe all these religions lead to you. As of today, I am no longer looking for you. But if you give me the truth about you, I'll live it.)* I lived my life no longer looking for God. The altar in my bedroom I threw it away. The paper with my ancestor's names on it, I threw it away. All the materials on the Orishas, I threw it away. I stopped going to see the African priestess, I didn't no longer called I had a job working with her boyfriend. He taught me how to make African jewelry and leather bags. I quit that job. I stopped coming around their family altogether for many years. I mentioned in my book, "A Pastor's

Mistake," when I found someone new to do my twist hairstyle. The person doing my twists was a member of their family. This was about 9 years later. I stopped everything and disconnected with everyone connected to Yoruba. I stopped wearing my African clothes. And to top it all off, I stopped praying to God, to the Orishas, and to my ancestors. I didn't pray at all anymore. I was no longer looking for God.

With no prayer of any kind in my life, I lived my life. I continued attending Hillsborough Community College. I played basketball with Clarence, Alton, and Alfonso. We balled all over Tampa destroying everyone we played. We had a reputation for winning. It didn't matter who the 5th person was that joined our squad. We still won. The 5th person on our squad was my new girlfriend after the African priestess daughter. This woman is in my book, "From Woman To Woman" in the chapter entitled,

"The Whole Package." We had our issues. I played video games with by my boy T. We were very competitive and got angry plenty of times as we played multiple games. In addition, I partied with 2AM (Alton + Alfonso + Marcus = A+A+M = 2AM) We had a reputation for dancing as well, we were very popular on the party scene, and some of this is captured in my book "From Woman To Woman." We will be writing our book "2AM" sometime soon. Well, I lived my life without looking for God anymore, and all was the same until I went to the beach one day.

Although I lived in Tampa Florida, I didn't go to the beach very often. On this particular day, some friends thought we should hang out at the beach. We didn't bring food or drinks. This was spur of the moment. I called up the fellas and those who could come accompanied me. We met up with the ladies and it was a fun time. We took plenty of pictures and our poses were very sensuous and erotic. As skinny as I was then, I was very confident that I was sexy and attractive. We took pictures with the female's arms wrapped around my legs as I stood up. They were all on the sand under me. They had on very nice bathing suits and I had on a zebra black white thong for men. It wasn't considered being gay back then. I wouldn't dare wear that now and they have all been trashed . I used to wear those things under my M.C. Hammer pants and sometimes the ladies acknowledged they could see them through the material. So I pulled the hammer pants down on the sides so all women could see them as I danced in the clubs. I'm shaking my head at myself. I was something else back then, especially when I was whining to Caribbean music. Anyway, a few of my boys didn't want to take any pictures because they didn't want their women to possibly see these photos at a later time. I had a girlfriend and didn't care because I believed she was cheating one me, and I was cheating on her. We took many provocative photos and I was loving it. Tongues out, licking lips, and mouths open as if they wanted them filled. We were very nasty and never did anything like this publicly before, but we had so much fun doing it. Then the ladies wanted pictures with me under them. I had my tongue fixed as if I was about to give them oral. They bent over and we did so many other poses. Yep, it was a very freaky beach day. No social media then or cellphones, but I had a good 35 millimeter camera with a zoom lens. I bought it with money left over from my student financial aid money. I didn't have a job at this time. I looked forward to seeing these nasty pictures. It wouldn't take long to get them developed at the "1 Hour Photo" at Eckerd Drugs. (Now CVS Pharmacy)

After our nasty photo shoot, everyone got

in the water except me. I couldn't swim and didn't want to risk it. I've been in the water before with my mom. We were in the Gulf of Mexico with mom's friend, Judy's boyfriend, who took us out looking for conch. We were up to our waistlines in the gulf. It didn't dawn on me until a boat went by us that I was really in the ocean. I was used to fresh water Lake Michigan in Chicago. As I pondered on the things in the ocean, I was ready to leave. My mom felt the same way and we both vowed never to do it again. At least we weren't afraid, but you don't have to be afraid to suffer tragedy. We were relieved once we were back on the beach and headed home.

Here's what happened to me. Two of my boys grabbed me, picked me up, and carried me out into the water. They were both muscular and I was skinny. The ladies thought this was so funny. My boys were laughing too. "You're going to get in this water today." "Yeah, stop being scared." A few statements the fellas made as they carried me. I couldn't believe my eyes as they took me further and further out. Then to my horror, they threw me. Splash! I went under and began fighting trying to get my head above the water. As soon I started to panic I stopped. Realizing I would drown if I didn't orientate myself. I soon discovered I could stand up as I coughed up water. I was so angry as they laughed at me. I wiped my eyes as I stopped still. After I cleared my eyes, I made my way back to the beach. I swallowed some water. How much? I don't know. As I made my way back to the beach, my stomach began hurting. I held it as I walked through the water. Out of nowhere, I threw up. It was some thick foamy looking stuff. The ladies were disgusted as they watched and asked if I was alright after I was done. I started making my way back to the beach and threw up again. It was more of the same. By the time my feet touch the beach, I had a fever. I laid down and hoped it would stop. It didn't. Twenty minutes later, I said to everyone, "I'm not feeling well. Let's go." We didn't have much to gather and we all called it a day.

I drove one of my boys home first. I had to really take my time as I drove. I was feeling worse as I pulled up to his house. I asked my other boy to drive because I couldn't. We stayed in the same apartment complex and when I got home, I told my mom I was sick. I grabbed some over the counter flu medicine and laid in my bed. As soon as I got comfortable, there was a knock on my door. It was Alfonso and Alton. They wanted to party and I wasn't feeling it. I fell asleep as they all played my Super Nintendo. When I woke up, it was early the next day. Everyone was gone and I was confused as I looked around burning with a fever.

I continued taking over the counter flu medicine and started drinking fluids. The biggest difference in how I was feeling was my throat was hurting very badly. I've had issues with tonsillitis before, and I believed this was probably it again. As the day progressed, my throat grew worse. I went to the bathroom to look at it. It was swollen and covered with those light colored patches. I had no appetite and hated swallowing. I rested and slept most of the day.

The next I took a shower because I didn't take one the day before. I brushed my teeth and asked my mom to take me to the Walk-In Clinic. This was a doctor's office that was on Busch Blvd near the bowling alley. You didn't need an appointment. My mom took me and the nurse took my vital signs. My fever was 105. My voice was weak and I could barely speak up. This was the worse my tonsils were every swollen. They laid me on what I called a bed of ice. It was supposed to lower my fever. This cold thing I laid on felt sooooo good. I was comfortable and rested on it as the nurse / doctor talked with my mom. I was given some prescriptions and heard them say, "If his fever doesn't break, take him to the hospital." We picked up my prescription and I took my medicine hoping I would feel better. I ate chicken noodle soup and dreaded the pain as I swallowed. I rested and soon fell asleep. I woke up right when it was time to take my next dosage. I immediately noticed I didn't feel any better. I took my second dose, and later the third dose. There was no change. That night I couldn't sleep very well and my throat was hurting even worse. I couldn't wait to go to the hospital in the morning. I was miserable and needed relief.

The next day, my mom took me to University Community Hospital. After they took my vital signs, saw the paperwork from the Walk-In Clinic, and saw my temperature was 105, they said they were going to admit me. I was so tired because I didn't sleep well the night before, I could barely talk because my throat so swollen. A nurse started me with an IV as we were waiting for my room. This is when my eyes began seeing things in the supernatural realm.

As my mom and I were in a small room near the emergency room waiting, I started hearing things, and I started seeing things. I was very skeptical about saying anything because of what happened when I was a small boy. I started seeing people who I knew, but couldn't explain how I knew them. They were walking up to me and looking at me. They were observing me with an interest that kept my attention. I soon realized who these people were. These were people I knew had died when I was a child. I don't know how I knew who they were, but I did. So, I opened my mouth and told my mom. At first she kept repeating that no one is there. Then a strong presence entered that room. Once again, I knew exactly what this presence was and I can't explain how I know. It wasn't a relative of mine or anyone who was human. This was death.

"Mom, I'm about to die." I uttered very sadly. My mom expressed with so much concern, "Maine, don't say that. Don't confess that." I heard my mom and sadly stated, "But I am about to die. I can hear Big Momma singing." Big Momma is my mom's mother who passed about 3 years ago in 1990. She was a Christian and sung many songs that I remember. I can't say I knew her very well, but I remember going to the store for her to get her favorite Archway cookies. She loved the Chicago Cubs and I loved letting her watch them on my 12 inch black & white television. When she visited us, she stayed in my bedroom and I was more than happy to give my bed up to her. I loved her visits and she moved in with us for a short time. Now I'm ill and hearing her sing like she did when she used to cook dinner. Even though I heard her singing about Jesus, I didn't believe in Jesus. I hated the bible. I was an enemy of the cross and didn't know it. I'm sure my mom was praying for me. She never liked me learning that African religion. She saw my altar and had a Jesus fit. On the contrary, when I took it down and threw it away she was overjoyed. My grandmother lived to be over one hundred years old. No one knew her age. Apparently she was born before birth certificates or she never had one. Somethings in my family I've never asked any questions about. There are plenty of mysteries in my family that I do not want to solve. I've let them all go. Yep, I'm over it. It's cool.

My mom asked, "What is Big Momma singing?" I was astonished she asked. "Jesus on the mainline. Tell him what you want." I responded. My mom replied with passion, "Tell Jesus what you want." I really don't know what my emotions were as I answered, "Mom, I don't know Jesus." As soon as I released those words, I felt what felt like a very strong sleep come upon me. I knew what this feeling was although I've never experienced it before. It was death. My mom started shaking me as my eyes began to close. I also lost the strength to keep myself sitting upright. My mom shook me as my eyes closed and I began to fall forward. I could feel her grasp me to keep me in place. It seemed like it was in slow motion. As soon as my eyes closed, I opened my eyes immediately in a very dark place.

My mom was no longer present. I stood alone. I could see myself as if I was looking in a mirror. I looked as if I was infused with rage. Both of my fists were clinched and my teeth were as if I was biting down on something very hard. My lips were as if I could start growling. I looked furious as if I was looking for a fight. I looked so evil as I stood in the darkness taking in very deep breaths and releasing them. I looked down. My feet were upon very wide grey brick. These bricks looked about five feet wide and five feet long. They had strong lined edges that connected to the next brick. I was looking around as I continued to breathe in deep and heavy. I could see only darkness and bricks as far as my eyes could see.

Out of nowhere it seemed, this monster appeared. It was standing in front of me in the distance. I screamed, "I'M NOT AFRAID OF YOU!!!!!" In my mind, this was just another dream and in my dreams, I've been beating these monsters for years. Could the rage I had been because I knew a monster was going to appear? I don't know. I stood staring at the monster and it stood staring at me. This one was different from the ones I normally fought. It was bigger. Very muscular. Dark hair covered its body. Its head had horns like a bull. Its face looked nothing like a bull. It had two very long fangs that went up from its bottom jaw which was shaped like a dog's mouth. Two shorter fangs going down from the top jaw. The longer fangs were along the outside of its upper jaw. It stood about 8 feet tall. Its upper body was much wider than its lower. The chest protruded forward in muscular fashion. It had big strong legs that looked like a horse was standing upright. Its feet were not like a horse. It looked mostly like bear paws. I couldn't see its eyes in the distance. It had thick ears that were like a dog listening to sounds behind it.

A minute passed by as we stared at each other. Suddenly, the ground started shaking and I looked around wondering what was happening. All of the bricks started falling down. I was completely baffled. I didn't hear the bricks hit anything. It's like they just kept falling. My brick was the only one left. There was nothing under my brick holding it up.

It's like the brick was floating. The monster didn't have a brick under its paws. This was the first time I was ever concerned. How is this monster floating? I'm stuck on this brick and I cannot maneuver. My concern turned into fear. As fear gripped me, the monster started walking toward me. There was nothing under its paws. I had nowhere to go. I couldn't run and I knew I couldn't fight. I was too afraid to try to fly. (I could fly in my dreams.) I knew I was helpless. I've never felt helpless before. As the monster drew closer to me, my fear turned into terror. I had no confidence I could beat this one. Then it started walking faster towards me and tears welled in my eyes knowing I couldn't run. Faster and faster, it shortened the distance. I looked around seeing nothing but darkness. There was no escape. I've never had to look for an exit before. When I looked back at the monster, it was now 10 feet away, 7…, 4…, 1. My eyes were almost level with its chest. It was bigger than 8 feet. I'm 6 feet one inch tall and I felt so small compared to it. Its eyes were red and locked on me. This monster had a grin as it reached for me with its right huge hand like a gorilla.

With a very deep inhale, I suddenly opened my eyes sitting up hearing my mom, "YOU SCARED ME!!! DON'T EVER DO THAT AGAIN!!!" I looked at my mom not understanding her at all. She continued talking as I looked around wondering what happened. Right next to me was that monster. "Mom, do you see this monster?" My mom didn't reply. Her eyes were filling with tears. "Mom, its standing right here. It's here to get me." I stated as a nurse entered the room. "We need to take Marcus to get some x-rays." I was taken in a wheelchair and she was very friendly. She seemed nervous for some reason. I soon began to think she wasn't supposed to be handling me alone. "I need you to sit up." She says as

I quickly told her, "I can't sit up very long. I'm very weak." "You can do it. Just sit up for a few x-rays and we'll be done." She states as if that was the key words to give me strength. It took forever it seemed for me to position myself like she wanted. She takes the first x-ray, then the second, and the last one. This is the first time I actually felt an x-ray. After that last one, I had no more strength. My body started leaning forward and I couldn't stop. She ran quickly placing both of her hands on my shoulders. My head fell into her chest, "No, no, noooooooo." She strongly whispered as she caught me. "I don't need any lawsuits." She expressed looking relieved no harm came to me. She assisted me into the wheelchair and took me back to my mom.

I had no time to ponder on that monster that I don't see anymore. Was it death? I guess it wasn't my time to go and that's why I came back into my body. Maybe it was a dream. I do have a high fever. Maybe I'm hallucinating. My mom and I sat together in silence for a while. She looked so concerned. My mom and I didn't have the best relationship. With her working from 4pm to midnight, I only saw my mom on the weekends when I wasn't spending time with my dad. Plus, I would go outside to play with my friends. We rarely spent time together. Now that we were in Tampa, it was just the two of us. When we first arrived in Tampa, I was in my bedroom and she was in her bedroom. We didn't have any living room furniture. It was supposed to be only for 2 years, but we stayed. One day I realized that my mom and I didn't talk much. I went into her bedroom, "What do you want?" she asked as I sat beside her. "Nothing. I just want to sit with you. How are you?" I asked. She was so surprised. This began the days of us talking and I no longer entered her bedroom when I only wanted something from her. The same thing happened with my dad. I stopped calling him only asking for stuff. I called to talk. I was mad at both of them for making me move to Tampa. Starting over was hard for me, but in a year, I loved Tampa and embraced it. I no longer talked bad about Tampa and how country everyone acted. Mom and I went fishing together. Sometimes with her friends and my friend Clarence. We went out to eat at Denny's most times, or IHOP. My mom was very good to me. Especially, once we started talking. You'll hear more about her in the book 2AM.

The nurse returned with a wheelchair to transport me. She told my mom that they are having issues finding an available room. They moved me into a hallway to free up that room for another person who needed it. My mom sat in a seat next to me near a nursing station. As we sat together in the hallway, I began seeing people who were dead again.

There was a bright light and the people walked toward me from the light. They all looked so peaceful and smiled at me. I had the feeling they wanted me to come with them. My mom who was watching me closely asked, "Maine, what are you seeing?" I told her. She didn't say anything until I told her about the very cute little girl who walked up to me. I've always wanted a daughter, and she was so adorable. She smiled at me and stretched out her hand. I told my mom what was happening and my mom strongly said, "Do not take her hand!" I shook my head saying no to the little girl. She looked disappointed. An adult came and took her hand. They walked back into the light and faded away. The light disappeared after they faded away. I told my mom they were gone. I laid my head on my mom's shoulder with my eyes closed until the nurse returned.

Several hours passed by from the time I

arrived at the hospital. We couldn't believe it was taking so long. When the nurse returned, she had a bed to push me in to my room. After I was helped into the bed, another nurse arrived saying they gave my room to another patient. My nurse was very frustrated. She moved me near a wall and went to find me another room. My eyes opened to see more dead people coming to me. This time around, they walked up to me as if I was inside of a coffin. It's like they were reviewing my body and paying their respect. I didn't tell my mom this, but she was paying attention and asked, "What are you seeing?" I told my mom, but I saw relatives who I knew that died. They came to see me. Many dead people I didn't know walked over to view me. I literally felt like I was a dead man. At least I didn't see that monster that came for me and I didn't feel death like I did before.

Finally, my nurse returned and she had a

room for me. The only room available to me was on the pediatric floor. I had a room to myself. Probably because I was 22 and they didn't want any children in the room with me. I was happy to finally be in a room. I wanted to recover from this illness. My mom throat was so painful. Every time I swallowed was excruciating. My girlfriend, "The Whole Package," (From Woman To Woman book) visited me. She only stayed 10 minutes. I was surprised she came to see me. I didn't see her much these days. I didn't bother to ask how she got to the hospital. After she left, my mom and I talked. We actually had a few laughs. They administered various medicines in my IV and I started feeling better. My throat didn't hurt as bad, but it was still very swollen. They must have given me some good pain medicine. As the evening drew closer, I told my mom she should go home and get some rest. She was checking on me around the clock and I desired her to get a good night of sleep. I told her I'd be fine. I wasn't seeing anything supernatural and believed the worse was over. I was going to watch the NBA Finals. (Chicago Bulls versus the Phoenix Suns) My mom hugged me and went home. I was very optimistic I was going to get better soon. I had an airline ticket to go to Chicago for the summer. I missed all of my Chicago friends and I missed House Music. There wasn't much House Music in Tampa. When I first moved to Tampa, there was no House Music to be found. They listened to Bass aka Booty Music. It wasn't called twerking then, some of the ladies really knew how to shake it. It took a year for me to start enjoying Bass, but I missed House Music. Caribbean Music became my absolute favorite. Nonetheless, I couldn't wait to get back to Chicago. I missed my dad, my sisters, and the rest of my family.

As my mom went home, I was very

comfortable as I watched the basketball game. I loved Michael Jordan and this was also my nickname in high school. Otis House gave me this name when I dunked during a game we played at King in our gym class. I thought it was a joke at first because he was a jokester, and I believed he was dissing me. He graduated that year and I had 2 more years to go. It turned out to be a compliment and that name stayed with me. The NBA game was very had my undivided attention. I sat up watching the game with no distractions. All appeared to be well until the NBA players started moving fast as if a VHS tape was being forwarded. I became confused not realized what was taking place. I closed my eyes and tried to take deep breaths. I was so shocked when nothing was entering or exiting. I opened my eyes looking for the nurses call button. I pressed it repeated as I kept trying to breathe. I quickly understood what was happening.

My tonsils swelled until they blocked my airway. I continued hitting the nurse call button. No one came. I had one thought, [I do not want to suffocate to death.] With the little strength I had left, I crawled out of my bed falling to the floor. I completed forgot about my IV. I was crawling to the toilet. I was desperate and was attempting to do something very desperate. My intentions were to rip my tonsils out so I could breath. I now believe that would have killed me, but if I did nothing at all, I still would have died.

I was half-way to the washroom when a nurse walked in my room. She walked in with a friendly greeting. I saw her smile disappears she started calling code numbers. I tried to say something, but nothing came out. I tried to gesture I couldn't breathe as an army of nurses entered my room. One was clearly in charge. Everything she commanded was done immediately.

They forcefully picked me up off the floor and put me back in my bed. I was placed on my stomach and my hospital gown was opened completely. The nurse in charge was calling out many things as I was held down by the other nurses. I was combative because I couldn't breath and couldn't talk. A nurse quickly put on some gloves as the other nurses picked me up off the floor. As soon as I was placed on my stomach with my gown opened, this nurse put something in my rectum. This is the last thing I remember as I had a strong feeling of going to sleep overcome me. Maybe it was whatever that nurse gave me. I'm not sure. I heard so much commotion as I closed my eyes in the controlled chaos.

When I finally opened my eyes, I remember having a strong feeling of exhaustion as I realized everything was dark as blinked many times trying to adjust my eyesight. I was confused as I looked around wondering what was going on. I didn't have on a hospital robe anymore. I really didn't see my own clothing, but I felt as if I had on what I wore to the hospital. My arms were hanging in the air. I tried to move my arms. I quickly realized I was chained to a wall. I couldn't remove my chains. While I was trying to figure out why I was chained, and where I was located, I began to hear whimpering. I turned my head to my right and noticed I was not alone. There was a white man and a white woman chained to the same wall. She was the one I heard. He looked very sad himself. I was more confused and I was thinking was another crazy dream. Right when I was about to say something to them, I heard a sound. Apparently they both heard this sound as well because they both started crying almost simultaneously. The sound grew louder and so did their tears. It was the sound of a group people walking; so I thought.

I didn't even notice at first, but we were locked inside a cell. When the cell bars opened, I instantly knew I was a prisoner. I wasn't ready when that group I heard walking entered the cell. It was a group of monsters. I wasn't afraid and wasn't worried at all as I watched them enter. However, the man and woman cried and screamed out, "Noooooo!!! Leave us alone!!! Stop!!! Stop it!!!..."I looked over and was still confused at everything. The monsters that entered were short and not scary at all. It looked like I could kick them like a football. Outside of the cell were the big monsters. I could see the one I saw earlier in the hospital. I observed these monsters take this couple away together as they yelled and screamed. Then this little monster walked over to me, "Marcus. We've been waiting for you." There was a small pause in his speech as our eyes met. There was nothing intimidating about its appearance. The other little monsters left with the couple and it was now just us. "Don't go anywhere. We're going to prepare a special place just for you." Then it started laughing at me as it walked out of the cell slamming it. It was then that all of my confusion instantly left me. I understood. I became sad knowing I was dead. I tried to escape from my chains and with all helpless engulfing me I yelled with every fabric of strength I possessed, "GOD!!!!! DON'T LEAVE ME IN HERE!!!" My chains broke off of me and cell bars opened.

I exited the cell and was running through the darkness. I couldn't see much as I ran and I was tripping over things I couldn't see. I don't know how long I was running, but I heard the monster I talked to in the distance. He screamed, "MARCUS!!!!! YOU'RE NOT I GETTING OUT OF HERE!!! THIS IS FOREVER!!!" I could hear them as I continued running. I finally saw a light in the distance. It was very dim at first, but it got brighter as I got closer. When I arrived where the light shined, I had to stop running. The light was on the other side and it was very beautiful to look upon. There was this a great distance between me and the other side. Once again, I had this feeling of desperation and thought, [This has to be a dream. This can't be real.] With this thought in mind, I backed up to give myself some running room. I was going to fly over this canyon, ravine, or whatever it was, to the other side. I couldn't see the bottom of it. It was pitch black as far as I could see looking down into it. I could hear the monsters coming. They weren't far from me. Their sounds continued to get louder as I mustered up the courage to run and try to fly over to the other side. I stood there hoping this would work because this can't be hell. I just can't be in hell.

As the monsters drew closer, I finally ran

with all of my strength. Just as I approached the very end, I launched myself with my arms up in the air believing I was about to fly. I went up about 3 feet in the air, and horror absorbed me as I plummeted into the deep darkness. Before I could scream, a big hand from the beautiful light caught me and placed me into light. As soon as my feet touched the ground, this beautiful light started to retract away from me. I began running towards the light as it moved away from me. As the light moved away, I was in darkness running trying to catch up. While I was in darkness, I could hear female voices calling me. "Marcus, come here." I looked over as I ran and it was an ex-girlfriend. "Come over here and fuck me. I need your dick. Come give it to me Marcus." I ignored that voice and then there was another voice saying something similar. I started getting frustrated as I ran through the darkness toward the light. I shouted, "God!!! Slow down!!! I can't catch you!!!" This beautiful light slowed down. As I entered this light, I had perfect peace and I had an intense desire to rest. I felt so tired once I was in this light and my clothing instantly changed. I now had on all white which glowed and radiated. Someone also in all white met me and said, "Follow me." I couldn't see their face and their voice was comforting. I followed them closely and I kept saying passionately, "I want to rest. I want to rest." The person in white who I believed was an angel answered me, "You're going to rest. Follow me." As I followed this person, we started going up a spiral stairway that was crystal clear. As we arrived on the next floor, there were babies that were wrapped in white who were resting. A lot of babies. They were all sleeping so peacefully. I kept saying, "I want to rest." as we kept walking together. The person in white stopped and said, "Rest Marcus. This is your place." I laid down on something near the babies. It was a floor that was also crystal clear. I fell asleep almost instantly and this sleep was so good.

I opened my eyes to find myself back inside the hospital. My mom was lying next to me. I couldn't remember her name, but I remember that was my mom. Then I thought, [What is my name?] I couldn't remember my name. I was hooked up to various machines. I had tubes in my nose and things inserted in both of my arms. The one that was inserted in my left arm was very uncomfortable. I was about to take it out when my mom woke up saying, "Maine! No! No!!!" I stopped and laid back down. I looked outside my door and noticed nurses were seated just outside. I was now near the nurse station. I was in a totally different room. When my mom woke up, I asked her what happened and when did she get here. She had tears in her eyes and didn't say anything. Later this day, my friend Clarence and Karen visited me. They looked so sad. I remembered their faces although I couldn't remember their names. It was 3 days later. I remember a nurse entering my room saying, "You're awake? Good. Get up and take a shower. You stink." She brought me towels to shower and I could barely standup. I couldn't believe how weak I had become. I had to be extra careful because of everything attached me my arms. The nurse came back and disconnected the one in my left arm. I didn't have both of these in my arms before. I walked very carefully to the shower with my IV. I took the time to look at my tonsils. They were still swollen, but not as painful. I still had those nasty patches. After showering, I was exhausted. I noticed I had several food trays in my room and nothing was touched. I started thinking, [What happened to me?] When the fresh food tray was delivered, I ate some of it with encouragement from my nurse and my mom. I didn't eat it all, but I did eat something. I didn't have much of an appetite. The nurse returned, attached the thingy in my left arm, and administered something. She added a new bag to my IV. She talked very kindly with my mom. I soon went back to sleep. I had a few more supernatural things that took place, but they are insignificant to add.

I was in the hospital a week. I missed my flight to Chicago. I didn't see the NBA Finals like I desired. I was glad the Chicago Bulls won though. I believed everything that happened to me was a bad dream. It was all because of the high fever. The day I was released from University Community Hospital was very memorable. The doctor entered my room. I didn't remember him. Apparently, he's been interacting with me. He asked, "What's your name? (Marcus) What's your last name? (Boston) Where do you live..." He continued asking me questions and he finally told my mom. "He's going to be just fine. He will not need a spinal tap." My facial expression contorted because I couldn't believe he said spinal tap. The doctor discharged me. As I was getting ready to leave the hospital, I put my underwear on. They fell immediately to the floor because I had lost so much weight. I was already skinny. Now I was bony; literally. My underwear didn't fit me at all. It took me a month to recover fully. All the details of what happened are in my book, "From Woman To Woman" beginning on page 180. Here's how I became a Christian which starts on page 189 through 191.

How did I become a Christian? Karen became a Christian and asked me to drop her off at a bible study. I agreed. I planned to go to a party that night that Karen was unaware of. When I dropped her off, she asked me if I wanted to come in. I declined. But, I heard a voice say "Go Inside." I started looking around and followed her inside an apartment; not a church. When I entered this apartment, we were greeted by everyone.

There was a conversation that was taking place that immediately grabbed my attention. This woman was telling her dream to another woman. I was paying attention to every detail. I finally interrupted her and repeated the details of her dream that she had already shared. Then I began to ask did a, b, and c, happen next. She said it did. Then I asked if d, e, f, happen next and her eyes got so big. She almost yelled, "You're the guy in my dream!" I replied, "And you're the woman in my dream." Everyone was in awe at what just took place. This woman and I had the same dream of each other. This is the only time I've ever had a dream of anyone and met them, and learned that they had the same dream about me. This dream talk kept me there longer than I planned on being there. The preacher was late, and as I got up to leave, he was walking in. He asked me to stay and I did. He preached some message on Adam and Eve. I personally didn't believe anything he just preached on. Remember, I don't believe the bible at this time.

This preacher began talking to me and declared, "There's something you're looking for, and you're going to find it. You wanted to be at some party tonight, but God brought you here. (My eyes stretched wide because no one knew about the party I wanted to go to but me.) That wasn't a man in your closet when you were a little kid, that was a demon assigned to destroy your life. (My eyes stretched wider because that was the truth. I used to tell my mom there was a man in my closet and he's trying to get me.) You see what I'm doing, you're going to be doing it too." He said a lot more about my personal life that I won't add. That information might be in future books. Nonetheless, I looked at the bible someone let me use for that bible study and said in my thoughts, [This bible is for real!] No one at this bible study led me to Christ on this night. I went home and gave my life to Jesus alone, but I didn't know the bible, I didn't understand the bible, and only knew what the church taught me."

After I became a Christian, I went to bible study every Thursday at this apartment complex. The minister eventually invited me to his church and I joined. This minister had the power of Jesus working in his life. This doesn't make him a perfect person, but what it shows is that he spent enough time seeking Jesus. Meaning, he's studied his bible regularly, he prays regularly, and has given Jesus enough quality time so Jesus can speak to him. No one in the bible was a perfect person who served God. Stop looking for Christians to be perfect people. I didn't understand this and the devil used this against me to help me hate Christians. A hypocrite is a someone professing to be a Christian, but is not trying at all to be better. They do not make any efforts to study their bible and work on their character. They just do religious activities with no change at all in their life. Now I understand the difference.

I became a Christian because Jesus orchestrated a perfect plan. He saved Karen and she needed a ride. He spoke to me to go inside knowing I am spiritually open. I go inside to hear a woman having the same dream that I had and we both dreamed about each other. How amazing is this? I would not have waited for the minister to arrive because I wanted to go to a party. The dream kept me there so I could eventually hear from a minister who can actually hear from Jesus. God used specific information from my life without the need of a ritual of any kind. God knew I would believe if this took place. What an amazing plan of salvation Jesus had for me.

I believe God let me out of hell because I asked Him for the truth prior to my death. I also believe my death was because I didn't serve the Orisha Elegba. I just started believing this during the writing of this book. My friends never did anything so reckless before and never have since. Who throws their friend in the ocean when they can't swim? This is evil. I'm so grateful God had a bigger plan for me than Elegba. God knows I have renounced everything in Yoruba, the Orishas, my ancestors, the rituals, the tributes, the offerings, and everything I ever asked them in prayer. Speaking of prayers, my mom later told me that I was praying to some names she never heard of during my time in the hospital. She still doesn't like talking about it, but she shared that with me in 2022. I don't remember praying anything in the hospital, but this happened during the time I don't remember anything; not even my name

After I became a gave my life to Jesus, I was tormented with demons. I no longer called them monsters after the minister said the man in my closet was a demon. I've fought demons my entire life, but never how I did after becoming a Christian. I had to sleep with the lights on because I saw things in the spirit realm which surpassed what I used to see. It was very bad and I was physically hit by one of them. This info will be for another book. I was tormented. Guess what? When I started writing this book, these same type of demons started attacking me again. However, I'm 30 years in now and I know my authority in Christ. Orisha spirits are in the marine demon family. I didn't share this information for unbelievers. I shared this information for believers. Believers need to have this for information purposes for everyone who's going leave Yoruba / Orishas to come to Jesus. Take authority over every marine demon when you're praying for anyone who used to serve the Orishas. I know someone who left Yoruba and gave their life to Jesus. All hell broke loose against them. They needed tons of prayer because they were tormented by demons and witchcraft. It took some time, but they are alive and delivered. They made it to the place where they now understand who they are in Jesus and now have the authority of Jesus in their life. Don't be afraid to accept Jesus. I understand. Believe me I do. Take my testimony and apply it to your life. Jesus is more powerful than everything you've seen and experienced in Yoruba. As these spirits approached me to attack, I stopped their attack with the authority of Jesus, and I slept well. The power of Jesus is greater and every spirit is subject to His authority.

Chapter Five

"The Salvation Of Jesus"

Jesus is the son of God. Jesus did die for our sins and He rose again 3 days later. Come to Jesus everyone: witches, Yoruba, satanic worshipers, celebrities, lgbtq, transgenders, people who had sex changes, gay churches (God didn't make you gay etc.) porn stars, bisexuals, rapists, child molesters, murderers, pimps, prostitutes, whores, players, cheaters, liars, drug users, alcoholics, , tarot card readers, drug cartels, sex slave traffic people, all religions, the homeless, orphans, widows, atheists, politicians, people who are genuine good people, and everyone else. Accept Jesus as your personal savior. This is why Jesus died to saved us from ourselves in our sins.

I'm not saying come to Jesus so you can avoid hell. Come to Jesus and learn about

Him. As you learn about Him, you will fall in love with Jesus. He will gradually change your life. Don't worry about what you're walking away from, just come to Jesus. Now hell is a real place. After I became a Christian, I read a book called, 'Divine Revelation Of Hell.'' I read exactly where I was in hell in this book. This is when I knew what happened to me wasn't a dream. I was in a holding cell. I threw that book across my bedroom and cried. Do not believe people who are saying hell isn't real. Catholics, there is no purgatory. Earth is not hell. Hell is a real place. Hell was not made for humans. It was created for the devil and his angels. The lake of fire has to be extremely hot so it can burn the devil and his angels for eternity. You don't have to go here. Come to Jesus and struggling is better than never coming to Jesus. Struggling doesn't make you a hypocrite. Jesus died for the struggles. There is the grace of God for our struggles and the grace of God is for us if or when we commit sin of any kind. Just repent and ask for forgiveness as often as you need, but stay with Jesus. Don't feel like Jesus can't possibly love you. Jesus does love you. John 3 v16. We must yield our will unto His will.

God bless you. Thanks for reading this book. I pray that you now believe that Jesus Christ is the son of God, and I pray that you receive Jesus right now as your Lord and savior. "Lord, I ask you to forgive me of all of my sins. I believe that you are the son of God and that you died for my sins. I give my life to you and I accept you now as my Lord and savior. I thank you for my salvation." You may not feel any immediate change, but your confession is real. Romans 10 v9 & 10 Welcome to the Kingdom of God. All of heaven is rejoicing. Luke 15 v7 Study your bible by starting with Matthew, Mark, Luke, John, and the book of Acts. Once again, Welcome to the Kingdom of God.

About The Author

Marcus L. Boston is the owner of Unfazed Publishing LLC. He's been a published author since 2007 and shares his entire life in transparency to minister to others. He is a Christian of thirty years and has written many books to aid Christians in their walks with Christ. His first book, "A Pastor's Mistake. What To Do When You Know Your Pastor Is Wrong," sparked a lot of controversy and criticism. Marcus was attacked by various Christians thinking he was using real names and exposing people with personal attacks. After these Christians discovered that all names were changed and that the book was written respectfully, he began to get some better reviews.

His trademark in writing is being very transparent. He shares his life in truth in an effort to show non-Christians the grace that God has for himself, is the same grace God has for them. He shares his failures in an effort to help others avoid the same pitfalls he experienced; especially those who didn't grow up in the church. His personal theme is "Making The Church A Better Place"

Contact Me

Would you like to book me for an appearance or speaking engagement? Would you like autographed books? Would you like to become an author with me? Please contact me.

info@unfazedpublishing.com

www.UnfazedPublishing.com

www.MarcusLBoston.world

224.762.2242